# Meet Me at the Well

A Year of Verses to Strengthen and
Nourish a Woman's Soul

Designed by Red Feather Publishing
www.redfeather.com.au

Printed by Lightning Source. Suppliers are required to be environmentally responsible using sustainably sourced paper.

For Avalon and Bella.
And All Women~
For we are all daughters.

# Contents

CELTIC SEASONAL VERSES

# INTRODUCTION

Meet me at the Well, Sweet Sister, there is nothing we cannot heal. And welcome to this book of strengthening and healing verses for Women. A book of Holy Wisdom and Nurture that has slowly burgeoned over 14 years.

Come as you are, and begin, one week at a time, to draw yourself upwards, outwards and beyond.

The Holy Well is a sacred place in both earthly time and space, and also within us ~ the Wellspring that makes us truly human beings. A Well or a Spring in the landscape has been either crafted by the human hand and Heart or by the beauty of nature. A meeting place for the powers of the elements, Elemental Spirits, and the steadfast dedication and devotion of our Ancestral Mothers and Fathers in its co-creation. This tending over centuries creates magical places that have further grown in power and essence, becoming a dwelling place of Spirit. Those in tune can feel its very potency.

Within us the Wellspring is eternal, our connection to the galaxy and our beautiful Earth, running deep with all that we need to grow into our fullness as Spiritual Women in Earthly bodies. With consistent focus and tending, this sacred place can become more and more illuminated ~ a living, flowing protection of all that does not serve and a place of sustenance where the Truth of who we truly are can sing out loudly in the World.

In this book you will find 52 verses ~ one for each week of the year. Each verse a container of Words to infuse your days, for Words are one of the most powerful tools we have as humans. And more so when spoken out loud.

This book invites you to say these verses out loud, for the breath carries Spiritual substance, especially when woven with Words of goodness and wisdom. Speaking out loud may seem uncomfortable at first. But when Words of integrity and Spirit are spoken in this way, they are heard by our own ears, our very bones, our Soul and of course, our heavenly support. All layers of Human life and the life of Earth are nourished.

Learning a verse each week by heart also adds another layer of power ~ in this:

Words become Medicine
Homeopathic Magic
For the Soul, the body, the mind and Spirit

Many of these verses are essentially a self-invocation or a self-blessing for the Divine Feminine within ~ spoken in the first person or the 'I AM'. They have grown out of 30 years of working with Women in Sacred Space and working as an Anthropologist in some wild and wonderful places. Some celebrate a Woman's life ~ the cycles and seasons that wrap around her path. Some are for connection, healing, to transform darkness, and a few are Blessings directly from me to you. You will also find that some are seasonal ~ celebrations of the Celtic Seasonal Festival year.

Start where you wish! Trust your intuition, your own wondrous knowing.

You may also begin with an artwork that speaks to your Heart or Soul. Beautiful art is also a power in itself, a doorway to healing and moving beyond human struggle. Please use the images as Spiritual succour, a meditation.

Gazing upon these colourful prayers on rising can empower your day and when taken into sleep can be a tool to transform anxiety, bring deep rest and to clarify, strengthen and affirm.

I would like to honour here the Wise Ones who have scattered their wisdom upon my path and as a group of mentors have together inspired, somewhere along the way, many Words shared here: Rudolf Steiner, Glennie Kindred, Carolyn Hillyer, Dr Edward Bach, Hafiz, Caitlin Matthews, Joyce Rupp, and John O'Donahue.

Thank you to Anthony Macleod, co-creator and Artist of this book, for his heartfelt support and of course for his deeply nurturing artworks. I honour the Divine Feminine and Masculine within him.

Penny

# THE ARTWORK

The images in this book are a soulful reflection of my interest in the inter-relationship between physical and spiritual life. I believe that colour works directly at a soul level in the human being, helping to enrich the emotional content of heart and mind. Colour is inspirational as an essential quality, and valued as a bridge towards connection, balance and wholeness.

These artworks were created with a variety of materials, their combinations often stimulating my imagination towards unexpected discoveries. Soft pastels, gouache, acrylics and oil paints have been used on papers and canvas.

These images can also be placed in a variety of themes that are close to my heart and were created with this awareness:

The Beauty within Daily Life: Appreciation for the design and usefulness of daily objects we choose to use and surround ourselves with.

The Comfort of Angels: We are not alone but supported and guided by Spiritual helpers who watch over us.

The Gift of Friendship: We are a witness and support to the journeys of others just as they are there for ours.

Making Music: Musical sound awakens and nourishes our very core, right to cellular and soul reality.

Cultivating our Garden: Our inner garden needs attention and work just as our home gardens do.

Nourishment and Nurture: We steadily learn how to best care and support our being on all levels.

The Quest to Become: We are gifted the experience of Earthly life as an opportunity for growth, joy and development.

I hope these colourful prayers bring you nourishment and support, as much as I have found enrichment and affirmation in discovering them.

Anthony

## Meet Me at the Well

Meet me at the Well Precious Sister
We will collect sweet, clear waters
And wear flowers in our hair
We will lift up our faces to the Sunlight
Streaming though ancient yews
And gather prayers
For the Mother
Prayers for The Great Mother

Place your hand in mine, Sweet Sister
There is nothing we can not heal
We will raise our voices in praise
Our hearts in devotion to Moon, stars and dream
And we will gather prayers
For the Mother
Prayers for The Great Mother

Bring your ribbon, your posies and your heart, Dear
Sister
And we will dress the sacred stones
Our bodies will sway to the rhythm of Her flow
A weaving of wordless Blessings
Our smiles will be our prayers, Dear Sister
For The Mother
Prayers for The Great Mother

## I Am the Light of Brigid

I am the light of Brigid
Receiving rest in her Silent offerings
Receiving illumination from her Hearth

I stir the cauldron that is my Soul
And kindle Star bright passion
To sew stitches of silver
Into Earth, heart and cloth
A cloak of Her quickening
Of prayer and healing

And in this I am luminous in Her peace

macleod

## DIVINE MYSTERY

I allow the Divine Mystery to
Settle upon my lips so that every word I utter
Is in Devotion
In Service

Threads that stitch healing into the fabric of the Earth

In this I become more certain
Of my path

I tread its meaning with softness
I walk its meaning in power
I keep its purpose
Alight with Love

AWAITING YOUR BREATH

With a song for the Well
And a ribbon of Prayer
I come into the centre of your peace

In my hands, a Star is cradled
I lay it gently at your door

It glistens with tender dreams

Golden
Humble
Fragile
Emboldened

Awaiting a breath of hope

## WILD EDGE WOMAN

I name myself
"She Who has a Large Soul Song to Sing"

I stand on the edge of the Circle that says
I am too much or I am not enough

I am Wild Edge Woman
With a dance so unique
So loving
So Joyful and
So wise
That the circling Sun above
Laughs at my rejoicing
And the Earth beneath my feet
Cradles me, supporting my Soul Song
In power and in tenderness

# I Am

When I am bowed low and naked
The flame of your presence
Seems only an ember in charcoal death

My heart keeps beating
Barely

And when I have laid on that parched
Forsaken Earth long enough
I remember to breathe

For I am the Breath

I remember to breath Spirit into death

For I am Spirit

The flame kindles

Ah! The Universe sings

It was there all along

## My Girl-Child

Today I care for my girl-child
The Maiden within that still holds the Spring

I whisper sweet words into her Heart:

"I am your Mother with a pride so strong an ocean
could part

I will follow your footsteps as you dance through the
wild

And remind you that I love you, my dear precious
child"

## An Embroidered Dance

Today I will wear the threads of my Heart's song
And chant their colours into the haunted places of the
world's emptiness
Worn as a swirling skirt of story, song and rich
textures
That have gathered in me from my life-long journey
and dreams

Its fullness will sweep the wayfarer's path clean

Sprinkling all who hear its call
With courage anew
With mystery's longing
And signatures of Magic embroidering the dance

## MERCIFUL HEART

May I be Blessed
As I walk this uneven stony road

May my eyes behold fertile fields
Where once they saw barren Earth
Perceiving each person as a radiant flower
Wearing the sweet face of Grace

Embraced by these Blessings, I will open my Being
To the gifts and wisdom that live in all I meet

And in this my Soul path is enlivened
My devotion deepened
And my merciful heart will reap golden Light

## At One with the Story of Heaven and Earth

I listen at the threshold of the Spiritual World
A chalice receiving sacred nutrient
From the fires of the Universal heart
I am magically quickened and
Begin once more to be co-creator
And at one with the story of
Heaven
And Earth

## All Encircled in Me

My Womb is potent
Fertile
Empowered with life force

As Maiden
It seeds vision
Breathes light

As Mother
It holds
Tends
Cares
And loves

As Crone
It guides
Creates
Weaves wisdom
Brings peace

All are encircled and stirred in this sacred place
My centre
My Wild Sister
My Wise Mother
My Weaving Grandmother

## LIGHT OF FREEDOM

When my crystal-clear questions
Embolden the Fire of Freedom
In my heart

I am set free

From self-constraint
From the fog of desire to remain small
And desire to play safe

I am fuelled to take bold steps
No matter how jagged the path seems

To stay clear
No matter how comforting it is to remain
Embraced in illusion

Spiritual authority flares in me
My Truth-filled heart is warmed and bright

I am aflame

# EARTH BLANKET

This Earth Blanket
I will sew together
Piece by piece
Stitch by stitch
Weaving in moonlight silver
Sunlight gold
And shimmer of Star

My hands will work as the Grandmothers do
Sure, strong and agile
Calling in rich red soil
Clear flowing waters
And white bone shell

At the East I will sit
Singing up new life, new Sun
Sewing in Morning Star
Making magic as I work

At the South I will kneel
Calling up crystal Truth, nourishing Earth
Stitching in the Great Mother's bounty as I work

At the West I will dance
Spinning up a vastness of clarity
Sewing in power of curling wave
And drawing in inspiration of water as I work

At the North I will stand
In stillness, making Holy
Breathing into my Belly the quickening of Fire
Honouring the Sacred Hearth within as I work

At the Centre I rejoice!
With the Grandmothers, I have journeyed full circle
The Earth Blanket complete
I lay it before me and beyond me
Enfolding this world
With peace
Love and protection

## Dialogue of Love

Oh Great Mother
Spirit Father
Teach me the Language of Love

May my thoughts weave a gossamer web
Silver threads catching my dreams
Always honouring the visions of others

May my words craft a shimmering Light in the World
And my actions leave only Love and Blessings upon
Earth and in hearts

May words soothe and sustain me in the chambers of
my hidden world
And create a harvest of gold in my Soul

I ask that each breathe be a Language of Love
Each word a gift of Grace

## Filled

Filled as my feet walk upon the Earth

Filled by the cleansing breath of the breeze upon my face

Filled by the lap lapping of sweet waters as I bathe

And filled by the gentle kiss of the Sun on my tender skin

Receiving

Receiving it all in my own true way

Deep knowing that I am a Holy vessel

Remembering

Remembering that in each infinite moment
Each Sacred drop of time

Is my Prayer

## Woman Weaves the Sacred

I live each day as a Prayer
Experiencing the Sacred day to day

In this I honour all things
Both mundane and magical
With my full attention
A grateful heart
And with my whole Being

These intentions weave a soft
Silken cloak of Rainbow colours
That I wear always
In celebration of my Prayerful Life

## Protection Verse

My heart shines a light so bright
That I am protected from all harm
All negative energy and all fear

I walk forward in my strength

I walk forward with a Sword of Truth
That gleams with the Power of Spirit

I walk forward with a sword
That gleams with the Power of Spirit

## FULL MOON BLESSING

May you hear the whispering of your Soul
This night
In quietness

May you find your Sovereignty and purpose
This night
In the depths of the mystery

Moonlight Blessings be yours
And heart's comfort guide your dreams

Let the veil of Moon Blessing
Surround, protect and guide you

As you bathe in Her Light
As you vision into her Love

And as you dance this golden night

# WATER, LIGHT, EARTH AND SKY

I am
The silver glimmer of tiny fish
Streaking through the Mother's waters

I am
The golden windows of light
That criss-cross Her flow

I am
The gaggle of young children running
Strong, confident in body
For they know that they *are* the wind

And I am
The swallows that swoop in delight
Catching the kisses of God
In the azure stillness

As
Water, Light, Earth and Sky
I work in the world
With loving hands
Heartfelt care
Steadfast path
And Star-led vision

## WOMEN WEAVING A COUNSEL ~ A MEDITATION

I see myself sitting under a half Moon
Forever in the balance of things

Present
Spacious
Sitting strong

I sit among a Circle of Women
Weaving baskets

Each unique

As unique as the Souls we are weaving within

Our hands are deft and sure

We gladly teach and help each other

We share laughter and tears
Memories and footsteps
We share shell, feather, grasses
Wool and bead

Beside me sits a young Woman
Open
Yearning and
Courageous

Opposite me, a Mother
Filled with creative stirrings
Overflowing with nourishment

To my left, a Wise Elder
Deeply understanding
All seeing

Together we sit under a half Moon
Forever in the balance of things

This Counsel, this Circle
Lives in me
As a blaze of light upon my grateful heart

## SACRED GARDEN

I am a Sacred Garden
I speak to myself in sweet whispers
As gently as the breeze caresses a perfumed rose
I speak tender words to my Soul
As kindly as the rainbow's end kisses the Earth

With every passing of Moon and Sun
My loving words nourish me
And like every seed that is bestowed
Sweet rain
Warm sun and caring hands
I flower
I fruit

With every passing of Moon and Sun
My Sacred Garden grows more colourful
Can withstand raging storms
And reaches upwards
Upwards
To the boundless sky

My soul at heart, is a beautiful flower that I shall water lovingly.

Macleod

## Amidst the Pain

Amidst the pain
As I close my eyes
Warm golden sunlight
Flickers prayers in the Silence

I am ignited
In You
Rewoven

A fresh new moment awakens in me

And I rise

I unfurl

Ready to bring prayerful intention to
Each breath I take

## TEMPLE OF LIGHT

I raise my Soul to the Temple of Light
Light that is the dance of my life
The Mother's Oneness
Sustaining all, carries me
Even when I no longer remember
The trees still murmur their prayers for my journey
The peaks of mountainous land
Continue to sing their litany of strength guiding my
steps
Sister stream sings Her messages from world waters
As the pearls of Her wisdom call to the shores of my
Soul

In a heartbeat
Or just one breath
I can feel Her
Hear Her
And meet Her
For each and every day the soothing echo of Her pure
voice
Constantly calls me Home

## FRUITS OF MY SOUL

I am part of the story
That furthers the human journey

Weaving ancient paths of Wisdom
With fresh-fuelled Truth and Freedom

Untethered by the past
Strong standing in the present
And visionary eyes cleared for the future
The fruits of my Soul are ripe and ready

I know the Unified Source within
I know the Unified Source in all

## Ribbon of Green and Gold
### ~ A verse for Lammas/Late Summer ~

With gratitude-infused hands and heart
I hold the first fruits of my dreaming and my visions

The fullness of my Soul
A Prayer for the ripe offerings
I now lay upon Earth's altar

The green of Her body
Now turns to gold in me
A ribbon of alchemy
Entwined with the colours of my life's footsteps

Through Her turnings
The Rise and Fall
Wax and wane
I lay in store these Sacred jewels
To nourish Earth and myself
As Winter's song calls

## TODAY I WILL SING

Today I will sing a sweet song

A song of miracles
Woven from words
Of Love upon my lips
Of light within my heart
And the wisdom within my day's work

## RENEWED IN BEAUTY

In beauty I am restored
My Soul quickened
Hand and heart rewoven
Rekindled by the Sacred Flame of Beauty
The hearthstone of life
The centre of the turning wheel
And I am able to offer my gifts once more
And play my part in the healing of the world

Macleod 06

## Luminous in your Peace

Dark Mother
May I hear your call

Illuminate the gold of my Soul
When I lose sight of my Star

Quicken me so that
I am luminous once more in your Peace

## TOUCHSTONE

I will anoint myself with Holy words this day
Words of kindness for my Soul
Each sentence a Sacred oil
That soothes and lights the way

Between worlds

A reminder that I am infused with the Divine
And that my brow, my heart, feet and hands
Are touchstones as luminous as a Miracle

## AUTUMN'S BLESSING

As my Soul is awakened by Autumn's call
I wrap my heart in a mantle of gold

Pure light will now rest there, sustain and keep strong
As I quieten my Soul, and sing descent's song

I will kindle my hearth and nourish my home

Keep Sacred Flame bright

As I journey towards the shadows of Winter's dark
night

## Dancing with the Grandmothers

I am the Centre
Holding the threads of crimson red
Weaving a spiral of connection
To the Grandmothers of Wisdom
And to the Daughters of Freedom
These woven threads are my Warrior Shield of
red and golden light
Threads that cannot be destroyed by darkness or
ignorance
But allow the untamed in me
To dance

## Sanctuary of Heart's Love

My Heart is a place of sanctuary
I listen to Her tender whispers
As She guides my dreaming path
Never failing is She in her unbounded generosity

And so I listen
To Her rhythm of Goodness

A pouring of the Spirit of Love

Her rhythm of Beauty

Each beat a harmonious gift
And Heart's calling for Truth

Her poem ever-changing yet steadfast
In the stirring of the starry heavens

I hear the music of that sanctuary's peace

Her every utterance rejoices and

Comes to life in me

## A ROSE FOR THE SUN

I lift the veil
That shrouds my forgiveness
And see that each old rage nesting in the shadows
Holds a seed of my Truth and Power

I lift each potent seed to the beauty of the white Moon

I bathe each wound in the mysteries of the Waters

A Rose for the heart of the Great Mother is placed of
purest cardinal red

A bloom of pulsating light at the feet of those who
have hurt or been hurt

The Veil transcends
Shame or harboured darkness
And is brought to Sacred rest

The illusion released
The rose carried now in the glow of Sun's truth

## Faith and Trust

As I feel my Soul move within me
I see the reflection of its glorious golden dance

My heart knows that the story of my unique Soul
Will forward the human story towards the Light

I rise up in this Light
And the Divine fills my being with peace

## SUMMER'S END

As the Ancestors lit bonfires upon hilltop and cliff
To mark the sacred turning of the year
I light a beacon in my heart this day

With every step I take
I expand my vision across the land
That is my life
And walk it in gratitude
Leaving a trail of Blessings

My offerings weaving a basket of generosity
That bring gentle healing to Earth and all Souls

## Shadows of Light

In the stirring of the Dark Mother's shadow
I enter the void with courage

Surrendering to the messages of the unknown

Emboldened

For Faith journeys by my side as my Guide and
dear Sister

Her lantern flickers bright Truth
Upon the walls I have built around myself

When ready they will gently fall away
And I shall stand strong without them

## Ritual Woman

As Woman
I am a threshold
Gatekeeper
A doorway

Guardian of Blessed space and time
I stand connected by Holy thread to all
Women
Who use Sacred tools of

Earth and Crystal
Salt and Water
Fire and Feather
Incense and Prayer

To sanctify change
To honour loss
Beginnings and endings

Together our feet dance our grief
Our voices sing our joy

And we celebrate
We let go
We welcome
We release
We Bless
We heal

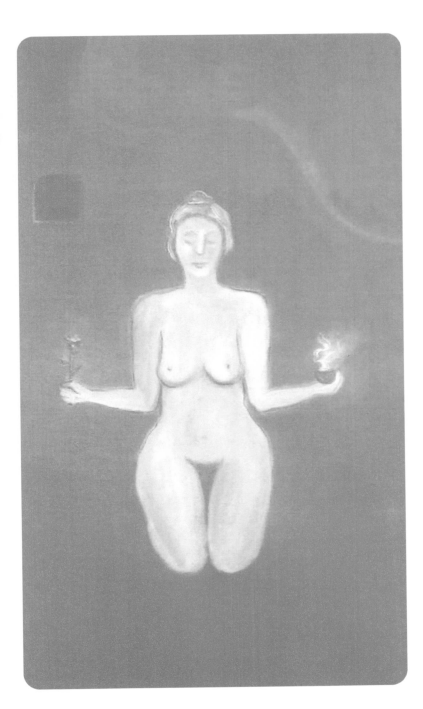

## I am the Promise

My feet stand as deep roots
Feeling the ground of goodness beneath
My deep thirst quenched
When I raise my face skywards
And hear the song of the Moon

A Fire is summoned
A promise is kept

Amidst the joys and struggles
That the River of Life brings
I flow

Awash with the rhythm of water
Around, through and beyond me

And I am the Water
The deep roots
The Moon
And the Fire

VISIONARY

I stand tall
Mountain high

I am Woman who sees
Beyond

I hold in my hands
Every priceless moment
Knowing within each
Lies a sacred space
That I slip into with ease

There, I Bless
My vision

I nurture
My dreams
I breathe a whisper of Prayer into
My heartfelt wishes

There, I stand tall
Mountain High

## GALAXY'S PRAYER

Into the gentle hands that hold the Moon
Entwined with the breath that stirs the planets
I slip into the Blessed Darkness

I become One with the stars
And dance the Galaxy's Prayer

When dawn calls forth
And the rays of the Sun
Kiss the Earth
I awaken renewed and ready
To tread my path once more

## CRADLED

Embraced in the gentle, steadfast arms of the Divine
My own breath breathes life into the embers of my
dreams

I shield and cradle my beloved vision
With protection, nourishment and faith
Knowing it will in time turn into Stars

A Fire flaming with Spirit radiance
Where longing, resting in grace
Will become a language that only I
Can speak in the world

## VERSE FOR A DARK NIGHT

Through the doorway of the dark night
Deep secrets and jewels wait to be revealed

A threshold opens to restore Spirit
As it awaits my crossing

Let the breath of the Great Mother
Guide me home

Let the arms of the Wise Ones
Hold me precious in a harbour of peace

As I journey towards the light
As I journey towards my light

## WISDOM WOMAN

With Grace
I watch all struggle and rejoicing with wise eyes

In the heart-felt moments I plant golden seeds

Seeds that will grow new tender shoots of Hope
In times of darkness

Seeds that will grow into strong
Lithe and blossoming trees

Trees of my remembering

Trees that whisper on the breeze

 "All will pass
  All will change
  All will come again"

## SURRENDER SONG

When I lift up my heart
And transform the need
To know, control or judge
I resurrect my whole Being
In a heartbeat

I hand over in Grace
And in its place Light shines
Illuminating my Sacred Gifts
The gifts that are the true foundation of my life

I weave them with the
I am

With the Infinite

I weave myself as Human Spirit

## THE SWEETEST RISING
### ~ Sacred Feminine Prayer ~ a meditation ~

As sweet smoke kisses the sunrise
She stirs the storm
As cold breath passes from her lips
She murmurs a prayer
And wildfire fingers weave
The thread
Back and forth
Past and Future
Canticle to the Grandmothers
Entwined with a Dreaming for the Daughters
A tide begins to swell
The ghostlike morning Moon croons
A high ledge, a new view
Sweeter even than smoke kissing the sunrise

## FORTITUDE

I call upon the unwavering strength of the Wise Ones

The Ancient Ones
The Gentle Ones of Heaven
And the holding Ones of Earth

May I be fortified in mind, body and heart

Standing steadfast in my Knowing

Constant witness to the foundation of my intuition

May my Trust in my Soul's voice be resolute

So that I ferociously protect my boundaries
And forever fill my chalice with Faith

BREATH OF THE UNIVERSE

As I breathe
I am filled with the light
Of the Universe

Beloved breath
Fills my heart

A glorious flame

Warming Spirit's home
In my welcoming Soul

## EMBRACED BY THE CIRCLE

My sovereign body
Walks a heavenly Circle

My body circling with the Moon
As She dances

I am

New birth of Spring

Ripe fullness of Summer

Golden harvest of Autumn

And deep Soul of Winter

All are held in a Sacred completeness

For I am

Woman

Complete and dancing

## Women's House

May I feel the Circle of safeness
The caring hands
The encouraging words of Friendship
Enfolded by my Soul Sisters to share my Sacred
stories with
Expose my weeping wounds to
And feel the healing balm of kindness soothe my heart

May my friendships build a Women's House
With solid foundation
Enduring walls
Warm Hearth
Hot tea and buttered toast
And filled with glowing faces

Mirrors

Mirrors that remind me of my Beauty when I have
forgotten it
Mirrors reflecting back to me the Miracle of who I am

May I forever feel the Circle of safeness
The caring hands
And encouraging words of Sisterhood

## Prayer for the Great Mother

Mysterious Divine Beauty
I lay my head in your yielding lap

Feel your hand stroke my brow
And your mantle wrap me round

I find enfolded within its folds shining Spiritual Truth

A place of nourishment

Grace and surrender

Where all my wounds, worries and woes

Are soothed, healed and washed away

## Welcome Home

I welcome the Silent place
Within me
Knowing it is a place where Wise Laws of Spirit
whisper

I welcome the place of Stillness
Within me
For there the breathing of Intuition can be heard

I welcome the place of Rest
Within me
Where my Soul
My Spirit
And my Being
Meet at a Holy threshold
Welcoming me
To step through a doorway of Grace
And to unite once more with the direction of my life

## Eyes of Spirit

In this bronze dish
Laid with Love
Are seven Stars

Each a burden
That I now lay at your feet, Oh Spirit

May I once more see myself
Through the eyes of your Love

And receive your Sun-illumined touch
Infused with that consecrated moment
When all earthly burdens and fears
Are swept away

In that exquisite moment
I rest in the joy-filled dying
When life is more Star lit than ever before

# PENNY CHAMP

As a young woman, Penny's Spiritual Journey took her to Glastonbury in the UK ~ otherwise known as 'The Isle of Avalon'. Here she spent much time over the last 30 years connecting to its powerful landscape and many diverse myths. The Isle of Avalon has shaped her life and work. It is from this rich and magical background that she brings verse, story, song, ceremony, ritual and Drum to her work.

After studying Anthropology at university, Penny was privileged to work with Women in diverse communities. She had the honour of working with Irish Gypsy Women in Oxford as well as West Indian Women, Homeless Women, Single Mothers, and here in Australia Indigenous Elder Women in the Pilbara and Gascoyne, deepening her belief that Women have a power within them, whatever their circumstance, to shine, strive, and change the world.

An interest in ancient traditions, initiations and ceremony led Penny to become a Marriage and Funeral Celebrant in 2008 and has since had the honour of guiding many individuals and couples across significant thresholds. For the past 7 years, she worked in a Steiner School, guiding Class 12 students through a substantial, powerful, year-long initiation process.

Penny never tires of working with Women in Circle and on retreats, witnessing them birthing drums, dancing, moving, creating, laughing, and resting. She is forever in awe of their capacity to love and support one another with grace and care, and to connect to the Divine within.

www.wildsisterwisdom.com

# ANTHONY MACLEOD

Anthony has been an art teacher and artist for more than 40 years. He began his journey as a professional artist in 1986 in Cape Town, South Africa and soon had the first of his solo exhibitions, followed by others in Johannesburg, Salzburg, Wellington and Perth. He also travelled, painting and selling artwork for some years in European countries, as well as teaching art in schools and in adult education in South Africa, New Zealand and Australia. For the last 15 years he has been a High School Art Teacher in the local Steiner/Waldorf School.

Anthony acknowledges the inspirational work of Rudolf Steiner as a profound influence over the many years of his creative and Spiritual quest. He lives in Rainbow Cottage near Fremantle in Western Australia with Penny and a cat called Little Boy and some bees. Here he loves to paint and play his collection of stringed instruments.
www.anthonymacleodart.com.au

Lightning Source UK Ltd.
Milton Keynes UK
UKHW051927210223
417424UK00001B/8